THE NEW
CREEPY CRAWLY
COLLECTION

BEETLES

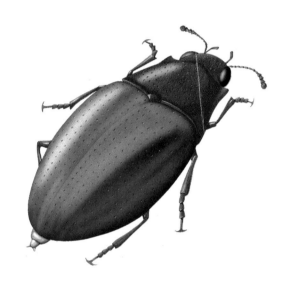

For a free color catalog describing Gareth Stevens' list of high-quality books and
multimedia programs, call 1-800-542-2595 (USA) or 1-800-461-9120 (Canada).
Gareth Stevens Publishing's Fax: (414) 225-0377.
See our catalog, too, on the World Wide Web: http://gsinc.com

Library of Congress Cataloging-in-Publication Data

Fisher, Enid.
   Beetles / by Enid Fisher ; illustrated by Tony Gibbons.
      p. cm. -- (The New creepy crawly collection)
   Includes bibliographical references (p. 24) and index.
   Summary: Describes the physical characteristics, varieties, and behavior of beetles,
as well as miscellaneous facts about these insects.
   ISBN 0-8368-1577-7 (lib. bdg.)
   1. Beetles--Juvenile literature. [1. Beetles.] I. Gibbons, Tony, ill. II. Title. III. Series.
QL576.2.F57   1996
595.76--dc20   95-54106

This North American edition first published in 1996 by
Gareth Stevens Publishing
1555 North RiverCenter Drive, Suite 201
Milwaukee, Wisconsin 53212 USA

This U.S. edition © 1996 by Gareth Stevens, Inc. Created with original © 1995 by
Quartz Editorial Services, 112 Station Road, Edgware HA8 7AQ U.K.

Consultant: Matthew Robertson, Senior Keeper, Bristol Zoo, Bristol, England.

Printed in Mexico

1 2 3 4 5 6 7 8 9 99 98 97 96

THE NEW
CREEPY CRAWLY
COLLECTION

BEETLES

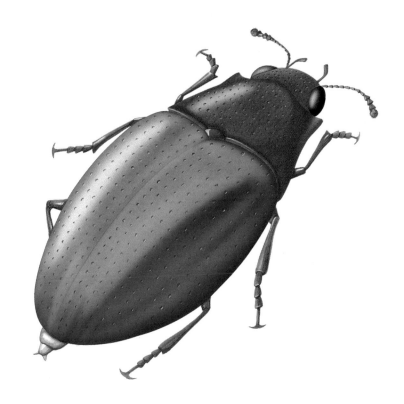

by Enid Fisher

Illustrated by Tony Gibbons

Gareth Stevens Publishing

MILWAUKEE

Contents

Getting to know beetles

This beetle doesn't seem scary. But sometimes you can spot a scary-looking one scurrying along.

How many kinds of beetles are there? What do they eat? Are they dangerous? Are they useful to humans in any way?

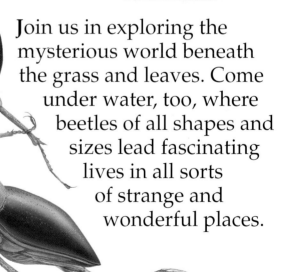

Beetles have been creeping around on Earth for two hundred million years.

But did you know that ladybugs and fireflies are actually beetles?

In fact, beetles are so common we sometimes forget to notice them.

Join us in exploring the mysterious world beneath the grass and leaves. Come under water, too, where beetles of all shapes and sizes lead fascinating lives in all sorts of strange and wonderful places.

Beetle bodywork

So many other creatures like to eat beetles that the beetles have developed a coat of heavy, bony armor to protect their soft insides.

Like all insects, beetles have a head; a thorax, or chest; and an abdomen. Look at the powerful jaws on this one's head; there are three pairs! Beetles use two pairs for holding their food. They then bite and chew their food with the third set, called *mandibles*.

Most beetles have good eyesight, but they rely more on their antennae for feeling their way around. These antennae are on the sides of their head.

The thorax contains the beetle's heart and is protected by a bony plate called the *pronotum*.

The abdomen contains the stomach, intestine, and respiratory system.

Most beetles have at least one pair of wings. Those that can fly have a second pair of wings beneath the outer, shell-like ones.

The top pair is hard and bony, and called *wing cases*, or *elytra*. The wing cases protect the delicate, fanlike wings beneath, which the beetle unfolds to fly.

Beetles have six legs, like other insects. They are attached to the thorax. Beetles that cannot fly often have long legs that are useful for running and jumping.

Beetle blood tastes awful to other animals. Some beetles can even bleed on purpose or squirt poison when attacked, so the predator won't bother them again.

The Goliath beetle, shown here, was named after the giant in the Bible story because of its extremely large size.

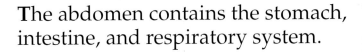

Hungry bugs

Some types of beetles will only eat certain things. Meat-eating beetles, for example, will eat slugs, snails, and worms for their dinner. Larger ones have even been known to make a meal of small animals and birds.

Sexton beetles lay their eggs inside small animal corpses. This means their babies will have a ready meal when they hatch.

Colorado beetles eat crops and can destroy a field in no time at all. They especially like potato leaves and may cause a farmer to lose an entire potato crop.

Furniture beetles eat wood, and thousands of hatching larvae can reduce even the largest trees to powder. They can also ruin household furniture by eating away at it.

Beetles of different types will even eat each other. Some, such as the larvae of stag beetles, will turn cannibalistic, eating their own kind. This happens if too many of them try to share a small meal of rotting wood.

Some beetles do not eat at all! They simply gobble up as much food as they can while they are larvae. This keeps them going for the rest of their lives.

8

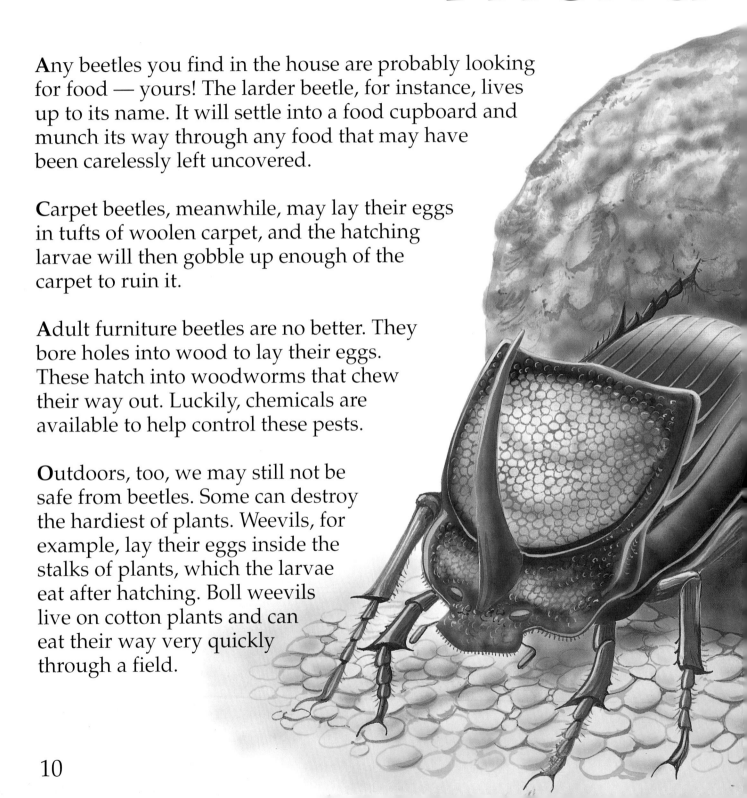

Friend

Any beetles you find in the house are probably looking for food — yours! The larder beetle, for instance, lives up to its name. It will settle into a food cupboard and munch its way through any food that may have been carelessly left uncovered.

Carpet beetles, meanwhile, may lay their eggs in tufts of woolen carpet, and the hatching larvae will then gobble up enough of the carpet to ruin it.

Adult furniture beetles are no better. They bore holes into wood to lay their eggs. These hatch into woodworms that chew their way out. Luckily, chemicals are available to help control these pests.

Outdoors, too, we may still not be safe from beetles. Some can destroy the hardiest of plants. Weevils, for example, lay their eggs inside the stalks of plants, which the larvae eat after hatching. Boll weevils live on cotton plants and can eat their way very quickly through a field.

or foe?

But many beetles actually help keep the garden free from other pests. Ladybugs — a type of beetle — are welcome in the garden because they eat aphids by the dozen.

Carrion beetles eat the rotting flesh of dead animals, which can help stop disease from spreading.

Dung beetles, as you can see here, will roll bits of animal droppings, or dung, into balls and bury them. This gets rid of the dung and also helps fertilize the soil.

Male and female dung beetles often work in partnership. The female does most of the work by digging a tunnel under the dung. The male brings the dung down to the female, which then pushes bits of it into specially-built chambers. The female lays a single egg in each of these chambers.

Moving the droppings is hard work, but the beetles can feed on them for energy; and so will the larvae, when hatched.

"**I**'m a bright red cardinal beetle, and I've just spotted some flowers at the edge of this woodland. Their pollen will make a wonderful meal.

"**M**y wing cases are on hinges that keep them open as long as necessary. My second pair of wings is folded up neatly underneath. They're so delicate I have to unroll them very carefully.

"**B**ut walk? Oh dear me, no! It's much too far. It will be much quicker to fly.

"**H**ere's a handy leaf that will make a good launch pad. I'll open my wing cases. Up they go!

"**M**y second pair of wings, made from a see-through membrane stretched over a big frame, is kept rolled up because the wings are so big. They need to be large in order to carry my weight.

wing

"**I** fan my wings quickly, until they lift me into the air. Now I have to keep flapping them up and down, faster and faster, so they keep me moving.

"**T**hat didn't take me long! I'm on the flower already. But I can't start my dinner yet.

"**Y**ou can sometimes see the tips of my wings peeping out from under the cases, before they are tucked away completely.

"**I**'m one of those lucky beetles that can fly to reach food, but some of my relatives have to chase after their meals on foot.

"**M**y wings have to be folded away safely first. This can take several seconds. I can lower my wing cases at the same time.

"**M**y larvae, which are a yellowish brown color, feed on wood. However, I prefer to dine on pollen. Now for my feast!"

Imagine what it might be like to step out into the garden and suddenly, by magic, find you are only 2 inches (5 centimeters) tall. Quick! Climb on top of this old piece of wood. It's a dead tree stump and bound to be safe.

But what's that? What a whopper of a beetle! It's almost twice your size and really scary. And look at those giant mandibles at the front. It's a stag beetle!

You are terrified it might attack you. But, amazingly, it passes you by. Where can it be going, looking so angry? Now there's another one, coming the other way. They stop and confront each other.

The action begins as the first beetle thumps the other with one of its mandibles. Then it does it again. But the other beetle is not taking that without a fight! Back it comes and knocks the first one over.

Unharmed, it gets up and attacks again. Now it looks as if the two are really hurting each other.

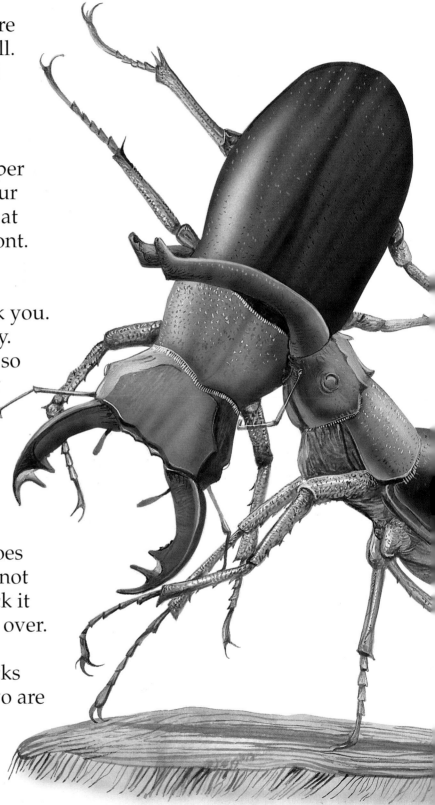

Beetle battle

Both beetles are "swinging punches," just like heavyweight boxers. Oh, no! The first beetle has knocked the other one off the tree stump. It's now walking away, toward a smaller beetle.

The smaller beetle is a female. She has much smaller mandibles, but they can give a much nastier nip and are stronger than the males' longer ones. Her mandibles are also more practical for getting food.

In fact, male and female stag beetles are so different they almost look like different species.

Now you know what the battle has been about! The males were fighting over a female. The first beetle just wanted to shove a rival out of the way.

There was no real danger, however, because their mandibles were too weak to do any damage.

Scientists have discovered that the males of certain types of stag beetles also use their mandibles for holding on to the females while they mate. The females may also be attracted by the males' large, antlerlike mandibles.

By magic, you are now back to your right size. How exciting to share the miniature world of the stag beetle for a while!

15

Ladybugs are probably everyone's favorite type of beetle. You can often tempt them on to your finger. What's more, according to legend, if a ladybug lands on you, good luck will follow.

You can usually recognize a ladybug by its red body and bold black spots. This is the most common type of ladybug, and it is known as "the seven-spot ladybug."

You are lucky if ladybugs choose to live in your garden. This is because aphids such as greenfly and blackfly, which eat plants, are the ladybug's favorite meal. In fact, as soon as a ladybug larva hatches from its egg, it can eat its way through up to thirty of these pests a day.

The seven-spot ladybug also eats the larvae of the dreaded Colorado beetle. Farmers who grow potatoes, therefore, often bring in ladybugs to save their crops.

ladybugs

The ladybug larva is dull and bumpy, not at all like the smooth, shiny creature it later becomes.

Birds like to eat ladybug larvae, but they will think twice about dining on an adult ladybug.

The ladybug has yellow blood, which it squirts out from its knee joints when attacked. It hopes the bird, or any other predator, will find the meal so disgusting that it will spit it out.

Not all ladybugs are red with black spots. Some are black with red spots, others yellow with black spots. Sometimes, you may even be lucky enough to see a white ladybug. This is a very young one. Its spots and body color take several hours to appear after it has hatched.

Ladybugs can fly and may come indoors in winter for warmth and a rest. If so, do not disturb them. They will wake up and fly away by spring.

Beetle

Can you believe that something as small as a beetle can have great powers? The ancient Egyptians did, worshipping the scarab beetle as a god. They thought it rolled the sun around the sky, as in this picture — just like a dung beetle will roll a ball of animal droppings. The Egyptians even made beautiful jewelry in the shape of beetles, and there are many carvings of scarabs on their pyramids.

Today, too, some African peoples still believe beetles have magical powers. There is one tribe, for example, that throws thousands of beetles into a lake as part of a rainmaking ceremony.

Beetles and bad weather seem to go together. In Germany, people once thought there would be a thunderstorm if they saw a stag beetle. This is because stag beetles like to feed on tall oak trees, which are often struck down in storms.

18

beliefs

Hundreds of years ago, people believed that sucking a beetle would cure a toothache! They thought that decaying teeth were caused by worms burrowing inside the teeth. Since beetles eat worms, people would pop a beetle into their mouths to try to get rid of the worms. Not surprisingly, the toothache remained.

Another old custom involved placing a beetle on a child's neck to cure whooping cough. This didn't work, either; but if the child got better anyway, people probably thought the beetle had been effective. Meanwhile, this only frightened children about beetles.

The powerful Medici family in Italy used the ground-up bodies of the Spanish fly beetle to poison their enemies. Its blood is very poisonous, and a single drop can make humans very sick. Eating a whole Spanish fly beetle can even be deadly.

The biggest family of all

Amazingly, scientists have described over 300,000 different kinds of beetles — the largest group of animals.

Beetles don't seem to mind where they live — in the deepest jungle, the hottest desert, or even the frozen North. The Arctic beetle can even survive temperatures of -75° Fahrenheit (-60° Centigrade). That's ten times as cold as your freezer at home!

They come in all shapes and sizes, too. The tiniest hairy-winged beetle is no bigger than a (.), for instance. But the great Goliath beetle can reach over 6 inches (15 cm) in length.

Some are round and shiny, like the ladybug. And the metallic wood-boring beetle is so lovely that people have worn it as a jewel.

Beetle legs and antennae are also different lengths and shapes. ▲ The longhorn beetle (*above*) has antennae longer than its body. ▼ The great diving beetle (*below*) has legs that act like paddles.

20

The great silver water beetle spends its life in water, coming up only for bubbles of air, which it drags below the surface to help it breathe. The rove beetle doesn't actually live in water, but it can jet-propel itself across a pond at great speed by squirting a liquid from glands located in its tail.

Some beetles are quite nasty to their enemies. The bloody-nosed beetle, for example, will turn around and confront its enemy with a squirt of blood from glands in its snout.

▼ The bombardier beetle (*below*) is also ferocious and will squirt out a boiling liquid 212°F (100°C) to burn its attacker.

▼ Have you ever seen a lot of little lights in a tree at night? These are likely to be female glowworms (*below*) trying to attract a mate. They, too, are a type of beetle.

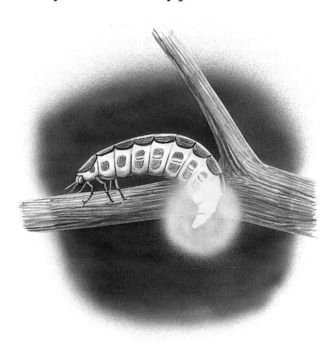

Scientists call the whole family of beetles *Coleoptera*, and new species are being identified every year. What an enormous family!

Did you know?

Can beetles live in water?

Many types of beetles live in water, but they need air to breathe. The beetles capture air bubbles between their legs and drag them under water. The bubbles then slide under the wing cases, from where the beetles can breathe in the air.

▼ Can beetles jump?

Some varieties can leap to great heights. The click beetle (*below*), for instance, frightens off attackers by flicking itself 1 foot (30 cm) into the air, while making a loud "click." The flea beetle can jump up to 2 feet (60 cm), over twenty times its own length. Just imagine being able to jump to twenty times *your* own height!

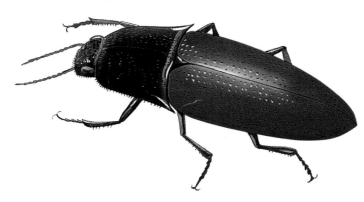

► Which beetles are poisonous?

Quite a few beetles are poisonous. The Spanish fly beetle (*right*), for example, can make you very ill or even kill. The arrow-poison beetle is also very dangerous and becomes poisonous by eating certain leaves. The Bushmen of southern Africa squash the pupae of this beetle on the tips of their arrows for hunting.

Do beetles eat each other?

Different types of beetles will eat each other if trapped in a small space together. Larvae of the same type will also turn cannibalistic and eat their own kind if there is not enough food to go around.

What are the main enemies of the beetle?

Beetles have many enemies, including spiders, birds, bats, frogs, and other small animals.

Is it cruel to collect beetles?

Beetles can live in captivity if treated well. Catch them in a plastic cup sunk into the garden soil, then gently put them into a covered container with holes. An old fish tank is ideal. Offer your beetle a variety of foods — insects, leaves, or old wood, for example. Release your beetle back where you found it when you've finished studying it.

▼ How are beetles born?

A female beetle lays many eggs, most often on the underside of leaves or in a hole bored in wood. The eggs hatch into larvae that develop into pupae before becoming fully grown.

► What is a beetle gall?

This is a kind of ball that some types of beetles build from bits of leaves. They glue them to a tree branch and then lay their eggs inside them.

How long do beetles take to become fully grown?

Some beetles grow from eggs to adults in a matter of weeks. But the stag beetle can take between five and eight years. One splendor beetle is reported to have remained as a larva for forty-seven years!

Where do beetles go in winter?

Many beetles die in winter. Those still at the hatching stage often stay as larvae or pupae and emerge as adults when the warm weather returns.

Are any beetles edible?

Some tribes living in remote jungles eat the larger beetles. The larvae of the metallic wood-boring beetle are supposed to be delicious toasted. Never try a beetle yourself, however, as many are poisonous.

Glossary

antennae — movable sensory organs, or feelers, on the head of an insect that are used for touching and smelling.

armor — a tough, protective coating.

cannibals — animals that feed on others of their own kind.

carrion — dead and decaying flesh.

glands — organs in the body that make and release substances such as sweat and saliva.

larva — the wingless stage of an insect's life cycle between egg and pupa.

mandibles — insect mouthparts used for gripping and biting.

pollen — tiny grains that fertilize female plant cells to produce seeds.

pupa — the stage of an insect's life between larva and adult; a cocoon.

snout — the front part of an animal's head that projects outward.

thorax — the middle section, or chest, of an insect's body.

Books and Videos

Amazing Beetles. John Still (Knopf)

Beetles. Peter Murray (Children's World)

Beetles. Barrie Watts (Franklin Watts)

Ladybugs. Sylvia A. Johnson (Lerner Publications)

Beetles. (Coronet Multimedia Group video)

The Ladybird Beetle. (Barr Films video)

Ladybird, Ladybird. (Public Media video)

Index